Table Of Conter

MW00627926

INTRODUCTION

■ How Better Speeches, Talks and Presentations Can Help You...

Walter Isaacson's terrific, best-selling biography, Steve Jobs, is filled with lessons about how—and how not—to be a visionary CEO. One section in particular is must reading for every executive who aspires to be a leader.

In 1997 Jobs had returned to Apple but was technically just a "part-time" adviser under then-CEO Gil Amelio. Amelio's place at the helm was in danger, but he was presented a great opportunity to rally the Apple troops behind him: he was due to be front and center at Macworld, delivering the keynote address before he introduced Jobs.

Here is how Isaacson describes what happened:
"Amelio had gone on vacation, gotten into a nasty tussle

with his speechwriters and refused to rehearse.... Amelio stood on the podium bumbling through a disjointed and endless presentation.

Amelio was unfamiliar with the talking points that popped up on his teleprompter and soon was trying to wing his presentation. Repeatedly he lost his train of thought. After more than an hour, the audience was aghast." [1]

When Jobs finally came on, he cut to the chase. "We've got to get the spark back," he said.

Amelio was gone before the end of the year.

Amelio's fate is a dramatic illustration that, even in the age of social media, a very traditional form of communication—one human being speaking to an audience—remains extremely important for entrepreneurs and executives. In fact, speeches, talks, and presentations are critical to three vitally important parts of your job as a business leader—winning clients, growing the business, and rising within the business.

Win Clients

Not long ago, the Wall Street Journal ran an article that started with these words: "Give a speech. Win a client."[2]

(1). STEVE JOBS, by Walter Isaacson, Simon & Shuster 2011, pp.307-308

(2). BARBARA HAISLIP. "RUNNING THE SHOW: The Gift of Gab " Wall Street Journal, August 15, 2010

And no wonder. The traditional one-on-one or small-group sales call must overcome some daunting obstacles. If you make a cold sales call, you can play telephone tag and talk to seven different people until you reach the individual in the right department—who may or may not be interested in your service.

Even when you get in the room with a prospect, you're that dreaded intruder—"the salesperson." There is a strong tendency for potential clients to tune you out. In fact, some customers shy away from having such meetings in the first place. They simply don't like the pressure of a one-on-one, especially if they're not already sure they want to buy.

If you're giving a speech or presentation to an audience that includes potential clients, on the other hand, the situation shifts dramatically in your favor. In a larger group, people feel less pressured, less awkward, and more willing to listen. A speech or presentation also gives people a chance to see if they want to work with you without having to listen to your sales pitch.

And, most important, the whole dynamic is different. When you give a speech, the audience is there because they want to be, not because you leveraged them into listening to a pitch. You are there not as "the salesman" but as a subject-matter expert, a thought leader. You're not trying to "get" something from them. You're providing them something they want—valuable information.

Grow the Business

While CEOs have always been the flesh-and-blood symbols of the companies they run, how the CEO comes across to audiences is more important than ever to a company's success. In turbulent economic times, critically important audiences get anxious. The groups most important to the survival of a company—employees, analysts, stockholders, customers, regulators, and the press—have to be convinced that the company leader is up to the job. Those key audiences want to know: Do the CEO and the leadership team have a clue about how to turn the company around? Do the executives and the board deserve more time to put an effective strategy in place?

Mike Daniels, former chairman of Network Solutions, former chairman and CEO of Mobile365, and former chairman of the Northern Virginia Technology Council, put it this way: "It's remarkable. If you have two growth companies headed by equally smart guys, where one can deliver an enthusiastic speech, lay out the mission of the company and encourage people to work smarter and harder and the other can't...it makes a world of difference to the success of the company."

Rise within Your Company

Because the ability to perform well behind podium has become so important to companies' success, executives who demonstrate early on that they can engage audiences have an advantage over colleagues who can't. In addition, good communication skills are relatively rare among senior executives, for reasons we'll discuss in this book. Speaking well in front of audiences is a great way to set yourself apart.

My goal in this book is to provide an easy-to-use guide for executives who want to leverage their personal communication skills to get clients, boost their companies or advance their careers. I begin by describing the challenges executives like you face when you stand at a podium. Then I provide some practical advice on how you can take your speeches, talks, and presentations to a new level. You'll also find examples here of how executives in specific industries have used and can use the spoken word to move ahead.

Finally, I conclude with lessons from some of the true CEO masters of the spoken word.

Enjoy!

SECTION I

I. The Problem and How To Solve It

Every man or woman who becomes a top executive has a lot of innate smarts, business knowledge, and skill. So why do so many do so poorly when they stand at a podium or sit behind a microphone? This section begins with one of my columns from the Washington Business Journal that tries to answer that question. Spoiler alert: one big reason is that companies don't realize how important communication skills are to a CEO's success.

Why Bad Speeches Happen to Good CEOs[3]

Former Sun Microsystems CEO Scott McNealy once said, "Communication needs to be a core competency of any business.

It starts with the CEO." McNealy's words certainly hold true in the economic meltdown we've all been coping with for more than a year. Business leaders *must* move the numbers, of course, but being able to communicate well through speeches and presentations gives CEOs the time and opportunity to perform.

Just last year, for example, Jerry Yang was forced to step down as CEO of Yahoo because, according to most outside experts, he was a very poor communicator.

Silicon Valley columnist Chris O'Brien articulated the conventional wisdom when he wrote that Yang fell short in articulating his vision to "the broader community that Yahoo needed so badly to win back."

At the very least, O'Brien argued, Yang needed to persuade "the doubters to holster their pistols and give the company a little breathing room...Yahoo really needs someone dynamic enough to stand up in front of a crowd and convert them by clearly articulating a vision and convincing them of the merits."

But what about now, when the worst of the meltdown seems to be over for the Washington region, and there are even some signs that the recovery has begun? As it turns out, top executives' ability to give compelling speeches is still critically important.

No matter how quickly the economy recovers, CEOs will still have to confront the fact that information available to stakeholders is little short of amazing. In an age of business Web sites, blogs, chat rooms, and search engines, all of an executive's most important audiences have instant access to information that was once the realm of specialists. Anyone with a computer and an internet connection can be part of an investor call, for example. At the same time, the new world of digital media also means gossip, rumor, and misinformation circulate more widely and quickly than ever before.

Information (and misinformation) is only going to become more widespread and immediate, even when the economy rebounds completely. That places a special burden on the ability of the CEO to communicate with key audiences quickly and effectively.

In addition, as the economy recovers, companies will be jockeying to attract the customers, investors and employees who were sent to the sidelines by the collapse of 2008 need. Their CEOs must be able to make effective sales pitches, articulate their vision, and rally employees wary about committing to a company that cut jobs not too long ago.

That also means that senior executives who aspire to CXO jobs have an opportunity – they can move out ahead of their colleagues by showing the board of directors and corporate leadership team they have the personal communication skills to lead a company on the rebound. They have this opportunity because few senior executives excel at public speaking, and many are terrible at it.

There are several reasons for this. First, think about the way most rising executives make their way up the corporate ladder. Unlike politicians in this city, most business executives move up through jobs that don't require them to stand in front of a podium or behind a microphone. They run trading desks; they are charge of large operational divisions, etc.

A 2005 *New York Times* story on CEO communication noted that as a consequence of this kind of work experience, a CEO's speech "can become heavily inflected with business jargon, with the focus on getting immediate results as opposed to articulating a broad strategy. Thrust into the limelight, where every word that they speak is parsed by analysts and regulators, the executives often find the transition jarring."

In addition, far too many executives are crazy about statistics. In fact, they are almost addicted to them. It's understandable: statistics are what quarterly investor calls are all about. Statistics also let an executive know how healthy the bottom line, how well a product or service is selling, how the regional economy is doing, etc.

The problem is that when presented orally to other audiences, numbers and statistics – especially when there are a lot of them – can put audiences to sleep. A CEO who wants to be effective, and executives who want to become CEOs, must find ways make the statistics pop and stick in the minds of the listeners.

Understanding why so many executives give such poor speeches and presentations is, of course, just the first step. In future columns, I'll offer some advice on what you can do to get better.

Q&Awith... Mike Daniels

I spoke recently with Mike Daniels, former chairman of Network Solutions, former chairman and CEO of Mobile365, and former chairman of the Northern Virginia Technology Council, to get his thoughts on executives' speeches.

Is a CEO's ability to give effective presentations important?

It's remarkable. If you have two growth companies headed by equally smart guys, where one can deliver an enthusiastic speech, lay out the mission of the company and encourage people to work smarter and harder and the other can't... it makes a world of difference to the success of the company.

One very specific is example the Titans of Technology speaker series we have at NVTC. When a CEO is the speaker, a great presentation is talked about in the technology community for a long time, but so is a bad one. A terrific CEO presentation tells folks that company has a real leader and someone they want to work with.

Do companies realize how important a CEO's communication skills are?

Based on my forty year business career, I'd have to say it's an underappreciated asset. While many organizations recognize how important speeches are, many others don't.

As a CEO and board member, has an executive's ability to communicate been a factor in your decisions on whom to promote?

No question that it has been a very important aspect of personnel selection. You need a strong executive who can communicate inside and outside the company.

The good news is that using the spoken word effectively is a craft, which can be learned through a combination of study and practice. The next five essays offer some very practical suggestions on how executives can improve their speeches, presentations and talks.

General Advice: How to Get to the Next Level[4]

Suppose that—like a lot of executives—you happen to be a mediocre speaker. You could be in for a struggle as the Washington area economy recovers. In a turnaround economy, the most successful top executives will be those who can make pitches and articulate a vision that will energize customers, investors, employees (and even the business press).

Now for the good news: you can get better. Speaking and presenting are crafts that can be learned. Here are six tips— four about style and two about content—that can get you on your way to delivering the kinds of speeches and presentations that can advance your company and your career.

Share your personal story. Relate some personal detail or story that illustrates the point you're making about your company's progress during the economic slowdown.

I've found that making it personal has two positive effects on executives' speeches. First, the personal touch engages the audience, making them pay more attention and strengthening their connection to the speaker because they can identify. Second, getting personal will fire up the speaker too, putting him or her in touch with the kind of spirit that moves audiences. Let's face it, we all love to talk about ourselves.

Use stories to make statistics memorable. When I'm giving general advice to CEOs or their communications staff, I usually just say, "Use stories, not statistics." The reason is that when presented orally, numbers and statistics can be sleep-inducing.

During times of economic transition, however, key audiences want some statistics—first and foremost they want a sense of exactly what is the bottom line. But the challenge is to make the statistics pop and stick in the minds of the listeners. You can do that by using stories—dramatic, ironic, or humorous anecdotes grounded in day-to-day reality—to illustrate the statistics.

Repeat yourself repeatedly. To deliver a good speech, especially to a skeptical audience, you have to turn off the voice in your head (probably that of your high school English teacher) that says, "Don't be repetitive." One of the toughest challenges for a speaker is to prepare something much more focused and organized than everyday conversation but to make it sound like everyday conversation. A great way to do this is to repeat yourself, using slightly different words to make a point. Repetition works because natural speech is much more expansive than the written word.

Don't believe me? Look at almost any famous speech in history, and you'll find repetition.

This is from Ronald Reagan's speech in front of the Berlin Wall: Freedom leads to prosperity. *Freedom replaces the ancient hatreds among the nations with comity and peace. Freedom is the victor.*

Conflict can be a good thing. Lee Iacocca became nationally famous in the 1980s for using speeches to save Chrysler. He once wrote, "A good speech, like a good novel, is constructed around conflict."

The reason is that conflict draws audiences in. If at all possible, draw contrasts between opposing points of view, describe how your company is struggling with another, how your division is helping your company overcome challenges, or find other ways to get conflict into your speech. It will add drama and keep your audience tuned in.

While style is important, it only gets you so far during tough times. Pay close attention to the substance, too.

Don't sugarcoat problems. It may be tempting to be less than candid when the news about your company's performance or your division's performance is bad. But if you're not frank, the true story will almost surely come out, and your credibility—with company leaders, employees, shareholders, the trade press—will be shot. Without credibility it's almost impossible for an executive to be effective, and your job tenure might even be at risk.

Have a plausible plan. Candor about problems is step number one, but as a recovery presents new opportunities, you have to be sure to present a plan for seizing the moment. A CEO needs a plan for getting back on the path to growth. An executive needs a plan for moving his or her division or organization forward. That requires a lot more than just saying, "I have a plan." You have to be sure your plan is detailed enough and realistic enough to convince your listeners it has a fair chance to succeed. Avoid vagueness, on the one hand, and don't over-promise, on the other.

Good speeches and presentations can help you seize the opportunities that appear to be on the way for Washington area companies.

Q&Awith... George Chavel

I spoke recently with George Chavel, President and CEO of Sodexo North America, to get his thoughts on executives' speeches. Sodexo (www.sodexousa.com) works as a strategic partner with 6,000 clients in North America providing comprehensive service solutions

What are some of the techniques you use in given a speech or presentation?

One thing I try to do is to illustrate a general point I'm making with a real-life story—something I've experienced myself or that I've heard about from a colleague. I find if I can relate to a story, I'm more comfortable presenting it and it is easier for me to connect with an audience.

How do you prepare for a key speech or presentation?

First I practice, over and over until I'm absolutely comfortable with the timing and the delivery. This is especially important for me because I prefer to use bullet points instead of a word-for-word script. I also make sure to have some of my colleagues—people I can trust to give me an honest reaction—listen to the presentation. I've even checked with my teen-aged sons, who I know will tell me what they really think.

How important are speeches and presentations to Sodexo's communications strategy?

We have a diverse and decentralized workforce of 125,000 and 6000 clients spread over three countries in North America. So we use every communications method and technology. But you can't operate a service industry without emphasizing face-to-face communication... everything from one-on-one talks with clients, to speeches to large groups of employees and suppliers.

Specific Action Tips

Starting Strong[5]

The most important part of a speech? For me, it's definitely the beginning. As Pete Weissman, an award-wining speechwriter and strategist who's helped leaders at CocaCola and other Fortune 100 companies, puts it, "The first few minutes are when the audience decides how closely they will listen to you, or whether they will listen at all."

There are two keys to ensuring those first moments grab listeners. First, the speaker has to demonstrate convincingly that he or she knows what worries, concerns or interests are on the minds of the audience. Ian Altman, an accomplished speaker and presentation coach who heads GrowMyRevenue.Com, says, "Every single thing a speaker does has to answer these questions: `What's in it for the audience; Why should a listener care?'"

Second, the first paragraphs of a speech should establish a human connection between speaker and audience. The opening moments should convey that the speaker is so likeable, authentic and interesting that the audience will enjoy spending the next 20 minutes or so with him or her.

Here are some ways speakers can achieve both goals.

- **Research, research, research.** There is absolutely no substitute for knowing your audience and knowing what is

on their minds. I try to learn every detail I can about where my clients will appear and the organizations they are going to address. Weissman says he makes it a point to find out what questions the audience might be struggling with. Research should include interviews with the event organizers, Web searches about the organization, talks with previous speakers, and just about anything else you can think of.

If you've done that kind of research, you can even start the speech by letting the audience know you know what's on their minds: "I know many of you are wondering how we can continue to grow in this changing market..."

- **Start with a joke (just kidding.)** Actually, telling a joke is almost always a bad idea. Not only do jokes often bomb, they almost always make the speaker sound inauthentic. Humor can succeed, with two provisos: self-deprecating humor works best; and only use humor if it is part of your personality and you feel very comfortable with it. "If you're not generally funny," warns Altman, "your body language will be uncomfortable, you tone will be uncomfortable, and pretty soon the audience will be uncomfortable...And you've lost them."

- **Find something specific that links you to the audience.** In addition to researching the big concerns of the audience, see if you can find an event, a person, a place that connects you with your audience. When I did a speech for a CEO who addressed the Detroit Economic Club, for example, he started by talking about how he "misspent" his teenage years as a gear-head

- **Lay the groundwork for the rest of your speech.** For an executive, a speech should always be used to move a specific audience to action – "buy my product, embrace our new business approach, hire my firm, etc." You should have that objective firmly in mind as you prepare your opening. You don't have to state that objective, but you should be opening the door to it.

- **Master your start.** I strongly recommend that executives know their opening cold, so they can deliver it very naturally and conversationally, without having to look at notes. That will allow you to wander among the audience when you start, and make eye contact from the very beginning. A "natural" beginning will get the audience on your side and make them want to hear more.

A great start is the first step to a terrific speech. In a future column we'll talk how to combine that strong start with a great finish.

Conveying Technical Ideas to General Audiences [6]

Speeches have a middle, too, of course. And one of the biggest challenges in preparing the body of a speech

(6). 2011, Washington Business Journal, All rights preserved. Reprinted with permission.

is figuring out how to explain technical material to general audiences. In 2011, I interviewed the CEO of the Biotechnology Industry Organization, who provided some terrific ways to deal with that challenge.

The Washington area is filled with corporate, government, and nonprofit organizations whose work is so technical, it's hard to explain to general audiences.

That poses a special communication challenge to the people at the top of those organizations. To gain insight into how to meet that challenge, I recently spoke with James C. Greenwood, President and CEO of the Biotechnology Industry Organization (BIO), about how he approaches speeches and presentations.

He put his challenge in perspective for me by noting that, even though rocket science is very complicated, at least people know what a rocket looks like. "Hardly anybody knows what it looks like when a protein enters the bloodstream to repair a genetic mutation," he said.

With a general audience, Greenwood doesn't even try to fill that knowledge gap. Instead, he keeps the focus on the impact biotechnology can have on patients. After all, almost everyone has been a patient, or has a family member who was treated for a serious medical condition.

He also searches out very specific details that illustrate what his industry can do. For example, he'll talk about biotechnology's potential to produce products that "prevent a couple from having to bury a child, or a man waking up one morning and saying to his wife, `who are you?'"

Powerful stuff.

When I asked him how he used statistics in his speeches, he said, "Sparingly." He noted that there are certainly some strong facts and figures out there that illustrate BIO's slogan: "Fulfilling the Promise to Heal, Fuel and Feed the World." But he said he'd learned from long experience that too many statistics make non-expert audiences yawn.

Much of that learning came when he was in politics (Greenwood served 12 years in the U.S. House of Representatives, and before that was a Pennsylvania state legislator.) "Explaining complex policy questions was something I did hundreds, maybe thousands of times in town meetings," he said. "My talks bombed enough times until I eventually learned what keeps an audience's interest, what helps them understand."

When we talked, Greenwood was working on his keynote speech for the 2011 BIO International Convention, held here in Washington this month. Although his audience will be biotechnology experts, Greenwood said it is still important for him to include dramatic details and stories.

"That speech has to be more than just a listing of events and accomplishments from the last year," he said. "There must be an inspirational side to it. No matter how hard bitten people in our industry are, they want to be reminded that their life's work is important."

To do that, he was considering a couple of approaches, including introducing BIO researchers who had close family members afflicted with a serious disease.

"In the end," he said, "no matter how expert the audience is, the best way to reach people is putting a human face on your subject matter."

■ Delivering the Bad News: Rule Number 1—Don't Make Things Worse[7]

One of my clients is the head of a federal agency facing serious budget cuts. And he is far from alone.

With federal deficit cuts, budgets are shrinking, salaries are frozen and layoffs loom. That means federal executives find themselves having to deliver bad new —often in end-of-the-year or start-of-the-year presentations to their workforce. There is no truly easy to do it, but here are some guidelines that can help make the bitter medicine a little less difficult to swallow.

- **Let all the shoes fall at once.** In a 2001 talk, John Chambers, CEO of Cisco Systems Inc., describes how he wanted to avoid the mistake of "dropping one shoe, and then a second shoe, and third shoe and a fourth shoe in terms of layoffs, or in terms of the business plan." In the age of social media, when not much stays secret for very long, it's critical for executives to get as much of the bad news out as quickly as possible. Letting all the shoes fall at once also earns executives credibility with staff.

- **Encourage action.** Fletcher Dean, executive speechwriter and author of "10 Steps to Writing a Vital Speech," says, "Make sure your presentation includes something that encourages audience action. Employees clearly need some time to absorb the bad news, but don't let them dwell there. Suggest ways they could trim costs or boost efficiency, or even suggest ways to talk with job counselors."

- **Make clear that you "get it."** That doesn't mean telling your audience how difficult these decisions are for you. Instead, use clear language to acknowledge the anguish, their frustration at having to bear the burden of a political fight, how unfair it is that they're subject to factors outside their control.

- **Above all, put yourself in their shoes.** Understanding the audience is always important to creating a successful speech. But it goes from important to absolutely necessary when you have to deliver bad news. Dean recommends executives work with a speechwriter or human resources professional whose specific role is to know the audience well and advocate for it. "Be open to suggestions," he says. "Build your messages around what the audiences need to hear, not necessarily what you want to say. It will force you to be more honest and transparent, and the audience will appreciate that, even if they dislike the news."

- **Finally, stay away from cliches.** A whole host of phrases can be dragged out for bad news presentations — everything from "when a window closes, a door opens," to "things seem darkest before the dawn." But even if you choose one perfect for the occasion, the message you give is that your sentiments are canned, not authentic.

That is one more way to make bad news worse.

■ Finishing Well[8]

In my last column, I talked about how important the beginning of a speech is, because during the opening paragraphs the audience decides whether or not to pay attention to the rest of the speech. I noted that, to grab that audience, a speaker must demonstrate immediately that he or she knows what's on the mind of the audience, and that the speaker is someone with whom the audience will enjoy spending 20 minutes or so.

But what about the ending of a speech? While the opening is most important, the ending is critical, too. Keep in mind that, to paraphrase former Chrysler CEO Lee Iacocca, the object of every important speech is to motivate. That makes the last words the audience hears from you critical to your speech's success.

Here are some ways speakers can engage and motivate their audiences through strong endings.

- **Start with the end at the beginning.** Everyone preparing a speech should start by asking, what result do

I want from my audience? What do I want them to do after they hear me? Then look at the way you plan to end the speech, and make sure those final words help achieve that result. That may sound obvious, but far too many executive speeches I've heard seem to end not on a high point, but when time runs out.

● **Bookend.** One of the classic and most effective ways to end a speech is to circle back to the beginning of the presentation at the end. "It can be a beautiful technique,"

says Angela DeFinis, founder of DeFinis Communications [http://www.definiscommunications.com/index.php], and an industry expert in professional public speaking. She notes that after a very, very long State of the Union speech, President Obama circled back to where he started, talking about the bravery of the Navy Seals. "It was moving and powerful," DeFinis notes. Obama got his audience back on track. And so can you.

● **Do something out of the ordinary.** Meryl Streep waved her Oscar for "Iron Lady" at the end of a recent speech introducing Secretary of State Hilary Clinton. She was making a point about the difference between playing a leader on screen, and being one in life. The crowd went wild. You don't have to do anything that dramatic, but look for an unusual quote (I found one from daredevil Evel Knievel), a little known event in history, a case of strange bed fellows, etc. Use anything that makes the audience sit up and take notice. One warning: as is the case for beginnings, humor can be very tricky in endings, so be very careful about using it. More specifically, don't finish with a joke.

• **Taking questions is great, but...** A Q&A session following your remarks can be an effective way to connect with an audience. However, you can't control the questions. That means you can't control which are the last words the audience hears from you. In fact, DeFinis warns, "That last question can lead your whole speech down a rat hole." Instead, she strongly recommends reserving a little time after the questions and answers for you to step to the podium and deliver your final, final remarks.

• **T.A.P. (Talk About People).** Try to end your speech by humanizing the larger point you're making. Find an evocative story or vignette that involves an actual human being doing something. The more specific you can be ("Engineer John Smith is on the front line of the data security revolution...") the better.

And Remember! Above All, a Leader Needs a Vision

Politicians and pundits have known for a long time that the most successful government leaders are those who are good at communicating a vision for the country. And woe to those like the first President Bush who neglect what he called "the vision thing."

Less well known is the fact that the ability to articulate a clear, powerful vision is critically important to the job tenure of corporate CEOs, too. In the long run, of course, a CEO has to improve profitability and (for public companies) boost stock prices. In the near term, however, the CEO has to be able to communicate a vision that resonates with the groups most important to the survival of the CEO's company—employees, analysts, stockholders, customers, regulators, and the press.

The vision thing is especially important in times like these, when CEOs of big-name companies are dropping like flies. During a single eight-day stretch in 2009, for example, CEOs bit the dust at Seagate Technology LLC, Tyson Foods Inc., Borders Group Inc., Orbitz Worldwide Inc., Chico's FAS Inc. and Bebe Stores Inc. Not long thereafter, Bank of America bid good-bye to CEO Ken Lewis, GM let go of CEO G. Richard Wagoner Jr, MySpace replaced its CEO and cofounder Chris DeWolfe, and the GM Board of Directors removed CEO Fritz Henderson. Here are a few things that CEOs who want to communicate a vision for a company should remember.

- **A laundry list is not a vision.** Just listing the changes the CEO is planning will not inspire anyone or convince stakeholders that the company is in good hands. I suspected GM's Henderson might not survive when he gave one of the most important press conferences in his company's history. It was supposed to be an opportunity for Henderson to communicate how GM would rise like a phoenix out of bankruptcy. Instead, all he did was list the things GM was going to do, using a litany of phrases that every executive uses to promise change—"a leaner, quicker, more customer-centric, completely product-focused company," blah, blah. As Phil LeBeau of CNBC wrote at the time, "How should the American public look at this today and say, 'We have confidence that this is, finally, GM's getting it right?'"

- **At important events talk about the company's overarching goals and describe how you plan to reach them.** Sounds obvious, right? But far too many CEOs don't seem to get it.

- **Appeal to our better selves.** The most effective visions inspire, moving employees to work hard, investors to stay the course, customers to keep buying. When Gail McGovern became president of the American Red Cross in June 2008, she faced one of the toughest turnaround challenges ever: the easiest problem the organization faced was how to close an operating deficit of $209 million within two years. In a 2010 speech last year at the National Press Club, she laid out the specific steps she was taking, but wrapped it around a new vision. She asked listeners to imagine "a new era of volunteerism and service where a culture of service extends from retired baby boomers to tomorrow's teens. The power of volunteerism is incredible, because through volunteerism, you can change the lives of others, starting with your own."

A terrific vision won't guarantee a CEO survives, but not having one makes holding on his or her job in a turbulent economy all the more difficult.

SECTION 2

II. How the Spoken Word Can Make a Difference

In this section we move from the general to the specific. The six essays here describe how business leaders in specific fields, industries, or situations can use speeches, talks, and presentations to boost their careers and grow their businesses.

For Entrepreneurs: What You Should Know about the Spoken Word

I have to say that I'm routinely amazed at how entrepreneurs struggle with their presentations to venture capitalists. The first two essays in this section bring together experts who offer advice on the structure and content of a pitch, and on that critically important, but often overlooked element—the Q&A session.

Pitching 101 – What's the Story?[9]

The era when entrepreneurs could write their ideas on a napkin and get funding is over. Instead we're in a very cautious time, which makes it more important than ever for entrepreneurs who get an audience with venture capitalists to be absolutely sure they have a powerful pitch. The easy part is the basic structure of your pitch. With a little web surfing or by talking to people with experience, you'll discover the handful of key areas your pitch should cover (the problem; your innovation, the market, your team, financials, etc.)

Then comes the hard part. You have to take these basics, walk into a room full of skeptical people, and convince them to give you money. Here's some advice, based on my work with entrepreneurs and the experience of pros who have been on both sides of the VC pitch.

You live and die by how you start. Whatever the formal length of the pitch session, a VC audience will be making a judgment about you in the first two or three minutes. If you don't grab them right away, it won't be long before they start checking e-mails on their blackberries, and your hopes for funding are dead.

"I can tell in the first minute whether or not to tune in to somebody's presentation," says Marco Rubin, Managing Partner of Exoventure Associates, LLC. Rubin has invested in over 50 seed and early-stage start-ups. "You absolutely have to get the essence up front."

Know your audience. This is one of the keys to writing a good speech, and it's even more important in creating a powerful pitch. Unfortunately, it's also the one that far too many entrepreneurs—especially in the technology sector—overlook.

The overarching goal of the VC audience is to find a start-up that has a good chance of yielding a great return on investment. Tech entrepreneurs, however, sometimes think the VC guys are like them – fascinated by cool new technology above all. As a result, the entrepreneurs often spend precious time talking about all the great things the technology can do, without focusing on how it can make money.

"Somewhere along the way, entrepreneurs who've developed a technology get so steeped in it that they forget to see it from the perspective of a consumer. They don't articulate a value proposition," says Warren Haber, Jr., whose sixteen years of private equity and venture capital investment includes serving Partner in charge of Mellon Ventures' New York office.

Image is everything. Venture Capitalists are really making two closely connected decisions at a pitch session: will this entrepreneur's company give me a great ROI, and do I want to work closely with this person for the next five years or more?

Conveying the image that will make the VC'er answer yes on both counts can be a tricky balancing act. On the one hand, VC'ers want entrepreneurs to have confidence in their own ability and vision. As Haber says, "They have a certain drive, a kind of charisma, the ability to evangelize people around a vision."

At the same time, arrogance and defensiveness will alienate the audience. "Even if you know more than the venture guy, he doesn't think so," says Stephen Kann, currently Managing Director of Irvine, California-based investment banking advisory firm, Bridgewater Capital Corporation. He has spent the last 20 years starting up, investing in and financing companies.

Don't neglect the Q&As. How an entrepreneur handles the Q&As can go a long way to determining what image the venture capitalists come away with. "A presentation is a lot more like speed dating than a formal speech," says Steve Fredrick is a General Partner with Grotech Ventures, where he leads investments in the software, security and mobile sectors.

That means the give and take of the question session is vitally important. To handle it well, you not only have to know the facts, but you have to come across as relaxed and casual as you respond to what's asked of you.

What's your story? In the end, a good pitch to a venture capitalist has to be a compelling. It has to have a beginning, middle and end, as well as some drama, and maybe even a little conflict. Rubin says, "Big funders want to hear a story that's fresh, that's engaging. Something like 'Before I came along the world had this big problem. Then I invented flubber, which can solve that problem, making the world a better place, and making all of us a lot of money.'"

Q&Awith... Khris Baxter

I asked Khris Baxter, a partner in Baxter Baker & Associates (www.baxterbaker.com), how he helps entrepreneurs prep for pitches. He and his partner, Brian Baker, work with business leaders and trial lawyers and are volunteer presentation mentors at the George Mason Enterprise Center.

What sort of stories should an entrepreneur tell?

First, the Eureka Story: the gap you've spotted in goods or services and how you'll fill that gap. It's your chance to tell how you're going to save babies, extinguish fires, capture thieves, etc. Then there's the Founder's Tale. Give us the passionate rendition of why you're doing what you're doing. Why'd you leap out of bed, run up the steps and kick in the doors so that you could stand before us and talk about your idea. Putting funds into a startup is high-risk. People who have their hands poised over a checkbook understand that tipping points depend on evangelists as much as they do an abundance of funding and excellence in execution.

What's your best advice for an entrepreneur prepping for a presentation?

Tear away the fabric of the business plan and the spread sheets to reveal why your naked heart pounds faster at the thought of how your business will cure what ails us. Everybody offers ROI and an exit plan. But so few people can explain why, when exhaustion claims us at the end of the day, we will be able to sleep soundly in the certainty that our day was spent not only attending to the bottom line, but, also in the pursuit of just and noble causes. Only your passion can convince us of that.

■ Mind those Q's and A's[10]

As the economy recovers, capital is more becoming available for new ventures, which means more and more entrepreneurs will be preparing pitches to investors. Successful executives who have been on both sides of VC pitches agree that when you walk into a room full of
cynical people to ask for money, don't forget your Q's & A's.

It's a 3-part process. "You've got to have three deliverables at pitches: a plan on a piece of paper, your spoken presentation, and answers to questions," says Marco Rubin, Managing Partner of Exoventure Associates, LLC. Rubin has invested in over 50 seed and early-stage start-ups. "If any one of the three is bad, you're in trouble."

Mark Ein, CEO of Venturehouse Group, LLC, and a long-time Washington investor and entrepreneur, goes even further, arguing the Q&A is most important piece. "I end up learning a lot more once the prepared part ends and the dialogue begins," he says. "When you start interacting, probing different areas, you see how diligent entrepreneurs have been in thinking through all the issues around their venture."

(10). 2011, Washington Business Journal, All rights preserved. Reprinted with permission.

Q's and A's and leadership. In fact, Ein believes that the ability to handle the Q&A well can be a good indicator of leadership potential. "Every organization faces a crisis at some point. So as an investor, your want to know that an entrepreneur can inspire confidence, can get people to run through walls," Ein says. "Part of that is being able to think on your feet, especially under stress. You can get a better sense of that from Q&A's than from a prepared presentation."

Q's and A's and confidence. The most basic way to prepare for questions from investors is to know your material cold. But there are additional things you can do. Khris Baxter, with whom I've worked on a few projects, coaches entrepreneurs and executives preparing for high-stakes presentations. He says, "Projecting confidence is key, so whatever question they throw at you, stay calm and cool. Know the material cold."

That's especially true when you don't know the answer to a question. "Investors know when you're faking it; they've seen it all," Baxter says. Ein agrees, saying it's much better for an entrepreneur to stay calm, acknowledge the question as a good one which he or she hadn't thought about. Then you might offer some preliminary ideas, or say the question deserves more thought.

Don't over-answer. Baxter also warns of the dangers when you do know the answer. "When people are nervous they tend to pour out every thought they've ever had about a particular subject," he says. "That turns investors off, too. Instead, listen carefully to the question, take a moment to pare down your answer, and give an answer that's to the point. It's that old axiom in sales: 'When you've made the sale, shut up.'" It's much better to have the investor ask a follow up, than to get bored.

Practice, practice, practice. Thinking on your feet, Ein says is "like playing a sport, where you get better at it the more you do it, whether it's in front of a large or small group. Baxter, who's worked in Hollywood as a screenwriter, says answering questions is like doing improv theater. "There are techniques you can learn, exercises you can do. Then have friends, family, and trusted allies fire off the toughest questions, no matter how off-the-wall." He says. "The more you rehearse, the more confident you'll feel when you're onstage in front of an audience of investors poised to write you a check."

Women Executives: Challenges and Opportunities at the Podium[11]

I hate to admit it, but I used to think that the challenges faced by male and female executives as they stood behind a podium were pretty much the same.

Wrong!

Some terrific women leaders, coaches and writers helped me understand that women (especially women executives) face special preconceptions and expectations when they face an audience. In this chapter, I introduce those challenges with the help of some women who have been on the front line of corporate communication.

As more and more women rise to the C-suite and other top executive positions, they have increasing opportunities to speak to employees, shareholders, customers and other audiences critical to their companies' success. At the same time, they are discovering that as female leaders the challenges – and opportunities – they face giving speeches are subtly different than the ones men confront.

Denise Graveline, a Washington, DC communications strategist who writes "The Eloquent Woman" blog, notes that women tend to be less comfortable speaking to large groups than men. She traces this to the fact that "During almost all of history, women were simply not allowed to address public gatherings."

Susan Peterson, who heads The Communication Center and coaches both men and women leaders, says reluctance to speak may also be due to the special challenge women present-ers face. "In trying to be assertive in a speech, women have to manage a delicate balance," she says. "If they try to take their desire to sound authoritative too far, they can come off as a scolding schoolmarm."

And to cope, women sometimes have a tendency to use what Peterson calls "weak speak": not only phrases like "sort of" and "kind of," but also "this may not apply to the topic, but...;" "This may be a little off target, but..." The effect, of course, is to undermine what the speaker is saying.

In her work with female executives, Peterson not only tries to get them to break their bad habits, but to use body language and strong scripts to develop what she calls "podium presence."

Both Graveline and Peterson point to one very specific challenge women face that men don't: clothes. As Peterson describes it, "Men could almost always wear the same suit and tie. Women have so many more choices, and they really have to think about the impression that choice is going to make."

Graveline noted that when Hilary Clinton wore a coral jacket to one of the early Presidential debates, she definitely set herself from the group of gray suited guys on the podium with her, which was a good thing. But, Graveline says, "The next day, most of the press coverage was about her coat, not her views,"

At the same time, women do tend to start with certain qualities that can give them advantages over men as speakers. Women are generally more comfortable sharing stories about themselves, especially stories that reveal their histories and even vulnerabilities. Every speech coach and speechwriter agrees that stories are the best way to audiences and move them to action.

"Speech experts talk about the advantages of an `effeminate' style, by which they mean a speaking style that is more personal, slightly more emotional, and more focused eye contact with the audience," Graveline says. She notes that three recent Presidents (all male, of course) who adopted this style are considered great orators: Ronald Reagan, Bill Clinton, and Barack Obama.

Kathy Clark CEO of SMARTHINKING, co-founder of Landmark Systems and former chair of the Northern Virginia Technology Council, agrees about the importance of sharing the personal in a speech. "When it comes to speaking, I learned by doing," she says. "Some of the best advice I got was to share my personal side. And every time I did, the feedback was the same: thanks so much for that."

She warns that, "Sometime women fear that, because we're women, if we share personal things, we'll be perceived as not being professional. In my experience, it's just the opposite."

She also says that negative stereotypes can sometimes turn out to help a female executive—when you overcome them. She tells the story of giving a technical talk to an audience of engineers in Japan, which was 99 percent male. "I was in my 20s and looked younger," she recalls. "You could tell these guys were thinking, `what is that girl doing up there?' But when I showed them I knew what I was talking about, it was like I got extra credit because they started out doubting me.

Clark also says that for men and women speakers there is no substitute for coaching and practice in front of an audience. "It's like any other skill. You wouldn't start out by trying to play 18 holes of golf. You'd take lessons, and practice first."

For PR Professionals:
CEO Speeches Can Be a Critical Tool[12]

Communication technologies are changing faster than ever. Still, executive speeches and presentations remain a vitally important tool for corporate PR. For this column

I interviewed the head of the Public Relations Society of America to get his thoughts on how PR executives can get the most out of the spoken word.

Generating more than $156 million dollars in the D.C. area, public relations is an important businesses in the National Capital region. Last month, the Public Relations Society of America (PRSA) brought 3000 PR pros here for its International Conference. That gave me the chance to talk with PRSA Chair and CEO Gary McCormick about the PR role of executive speeches in an era when communication technologies are changing at jaw dropping speed. (McCormick is, Director, Partnership Development, with HGTV, Scripps Networks in Knoxville, TN).

PR more important than ever. McCormick began by saying that both academic studies and anecdotal evidence make clear that, even during recent economic crisis, PR has become more important than ever to the leaders of businesses and other organizations. "Executives are embracing PR because we help them build lasting relationships, keep reputations during downturns, and hold on to good customers," he said.

He added that, while CEO speeches remain a crucial PR tool, it's more important than ever that they be part of an integrated communications strategy. "The CEO sets out the organization's positions and messages, but they have to be coordinated among both the internal `publics' and external audiences."

As an example, McCormick noted that corporate speechwriters often report directly to the CEO. To give the CEO the most value, however, the speechwriters should work closely with the PR staff to understand who the audience is for the speech, and what specific messages to that particular audience will serve the organization's interests.

The need for metrics. McCormick also pointed out that PR professionals are paying more attention that ever to developing ways to measure the impact of outreach efforts. CEO's would be well advised to make use of such metrics to ensure their speeches get the most bang for the buck, too. "The goal is to determine how much impact a speech has: does it generate buzz about the company, how does it effect the company's reputation," McCormick said. "Compiling those kinds of measurements can improve the process the company uses for deciding on the best audience for a CEO speech, as well as the best messages, and maybe even the best messenger."

Fragmentation and transparency. Turning to the impact of social media, McCormick noted that in at least one way, the revolutionary communication changes had actually increased the importance of speeches or presentations by executives – even though they are among the most old school forms of communication.

"The rise of blogs," he said, "And the fact that more and more companies are actually encouraging their employees to use social media, means that any company can suddenly become transparent. In addition, the explosion of financial information on the Web means anybody with stock has access to information only the institutional investors used to have."

"And finally, the media has simply been fragmented – segregated by political bias, divided up by age, demographic group, etc."

A speech or presentation by a key executive can a powerful way to get key messages out during this era of transparency and the media fragmentation. There are two keys to success, McCormick said. First, PR professionals absolutely have to stay on top of the dizzying changes in communication technology. "PR professionals have to remember that every time the media change, our whole industry has to change," he said.

What a speech can do. In addition, industry leaders have to work closely with their PR professionals to determine how best to leverage a speech. A speech by the CEO can be a terrific way to squash rumors or false charges. But there may be times when a CEO blog is more important. There may be some cases when the CEO is not the best one to give a presentation to a certain audience, or speak to a particular media outlet.

In sum, he said, "PR pros help executives understand today's circles of influence, and help them match the right message to the right media."

For Association Executives: If You Want to Lead, Develop Your Speaking Skills[13]

To learn more about how association leaders can use speeches and presentations, I interviewed John H. Graham IV, CEO of ASAE, the association that represents 22,000 association executives and association industry partners. In this chapter he talks about the links between the ability to speak well and the ability to lead.

It is no coincidence that ASAE, the association that represents 22,000 association executives and association industry partners, is headquartered here in Washington, DC. The association business is big business in the National Capitol region. Nearly one in ten workers in D.C. works for an association, for example.

Last month I sat down with ASAE's President and CEO John H. Graham, IV CAE to talk about how important speeches and presentations are for the leaders of his industry.

"The short answer," Graham said, "is that they are extraordinarily important, because communication is the most important thing a CEO does." In particular, he added, an association executive has to be able to reach three key audiences through the spoken word: People outside the association (the public, other groups in the association's particular industry, other association leaders, etc.), association members and leaders, and association staff.

To connect with these audiences, Graham said, executives should be as "fire-side-chat-like" as possible. That, he explained, means keeping things simple, being succinct, and backing up all points with stories and examples.

Still, each of the key audiences has its particular needs. From boards, he said, executives are usually looking for a specific result or action. An executive is usually making a formal, prepared presentation and should take great care that the arguments and the choices are presented clearly.

With staff, the irony is that the advent of email, social networking and other digital media had made personal communications more important than ever. "Staff want that personal connection, evidence that they matter to association leadership," he said. "They also want honesty, candor and transparency, and are very skeptical when they don't think they're getting that."

Those qualities must be in a speech or presentation because one of an association leaders most critical jobs is to motivate. That's true even when times are tough, and the news might be bad. "There is no way to pretend that a staff layoff is good news," Graham says. "But by being frank, and by linking that news to what the association will do going forward, you can still keep staff and members motivated."

That led me to ask Graham about how important it was for an association leader to articulate a vision. Interestingly, Graham said he thought vision wasn't as important as some made it out to be. "A vision is important, but it's kind of like the icing on the cake," he said. He explained that most of the time association staff and stakeholders want more tangible information about what the association is doing. How is the association helping its members do their jobs, improve their profession, achieve their goals, etc?

Asked about the impact of new communication technologies on speeches and presentations, Graham replied, "The biggest change I've seen in my forty years in association life is that speeches and statements are much more widely and quickly noticed that ever before."

To illustrate, he said that at ASAE's annual meeting he was on a panel with volunteer leaders. Joy Behar, the comedian, was interviewing the panel and she asked the volunteers how they could increase their salaries. Graham joked that they could "pay me more money." The remark got a laugh and everyone understood it as a joke.

Twenty or even ten years ago, Graham's words would have died there. Instead they rocketed around the web, and raised some hackles. "You have to be careful," he said ruefully. "Because the new technology can make the gap between intent and impact much wider than ever."

Over all, Graham said, he advised association executives who want to lead organizations to develop their speaking skills. "There is no question that the ability of an executive to present ideas concisely and articulately is essential to their success and the success of their organization."

■ Government Contractors:
Using the Spoken Word to Succeed. [14]

Not knowing the government contracting space well, I assumed that government contracting firms didn't need to be too concerned with their executives' performance at a podium. In 2010, two successful CEOs set me right.

My involvement in government contracting has been very limited. That's probably why until recently I thought speeches and presentations weren't that important for executives in that space. A couple of dynamic corporate leaders have set me straight.

Since 2008, Tim Dowd has been the CEO of Input, which helps companies develop business with federal, state and local governments by providing services that include market intelligence, consulting and training. Input also helps public sector organizations find outside support.

Dowd says his speeches have proved to be an extremely effective way not only to reach current and prospective clients but also to communicate inside Input.

"I can say things at staff meetings, but the organization tends to react more to things I say publicly than internally," he say. "The message often has more power when people hear me say it at a public event or see it in the press."

When he became CEO, Dowd used every speech and presentation to drive home the message that Input delivers high quality and that its members value the insight and service. As that message permeated the organization, confidence rose, followed by increased revenue.

Dowd says he learned an important lesson about presentations at General Electric Co., where he began his career: There is no such thing as a routine speech. "Jack Welch used every speech and presentation he gave to communicate the company's core values and most important themes," Dowd says.

Kevin Parker, CEO of Deltek Inc., agrees that speeches and presentations are a powerful way to reach government contractors. Deltek provides enterprise software for project-driven businesses, and its customers include many of the nation's largest government contractors. "Twenty years ago you might have been able to communicate with customers by memo, but now the government contractors we work with want that sense of personal connection, and a presentation by a human being is an important way to create that," Parker says.

As an example, Parker cites his company's annual Insight conference, which brings together thousands of its government contracting customers to network, hear about new Deltek products and provide feedback to the company. Parker gives the keynote every year, and Deltek professionals lead many of the 400 breakout sessions.

Although contracting can get very technical, Parker and Dowd do not use their speeches to present technical information.

"I'm not a deep technical guy." Parker says. "But one of the skills I do have is the ability to take something very complex and distill it down. I can explain it in a way that will resonate with a large group of people so a complex idea becomes a compelling idea."

One of the ways he does that is by telling stories. "As soon as I get off the stage after my Insight keynote, I start collecting stories and anecdotes from our customers to weave into next year's speech," Parker says.

He and Dowd both say it's important to make a presentation as much like a conversation as possible.

"The biggest thing in getting people involved is to have a conversational style," Dowd says. "I'm lucky because it seems to come naturally to me. For me, the best way to support that style is to storyboard my speeches, not write them out. The result may be that I leave out a key point once in a while, but I'd rather have that happen than give a wooden presentation."

SECTION 3

III. Learn from the Best: How Top CEO Communicators Do It

A few CEOs have set the standard for the best ways to use the spoken word to advance their organizations. The essays in this section offer some lessons from these world-class CEO communicators.

Lee Iacocca: Behind His Success at the Microphone

Lee Iacocca, former head of Chrysler, was certainly the first and arguably the biggest CEO "rock star." Yes, Bill Gates and Steve Jobs have also gained multimedia fame far beyond the business world. But no other corporate leader has scored the pop culture quad-fecta of being a category on Jeopardy, guest starring on Miami Vice, being the answer to a clue in the New York Times crossword puzzle, and getting assassinated in The Watchmen movie (okay, it was a look-alike actor playing Iacocca). Iacocca's autobiography was a world best-seller. And, in 1988, there was also a strong "draft Iacocca for president" movement.

Iacocca's business success—saving Chrysler and reinvigorating the American automobile industry in the 1980s—has also become a staple of B-school "case studies." And most analysts agree a key ingredient—what Iacocca himself called "my most important management tool"—was the spoken word. "I used that tool everyday," he wrote.

To better understand how he used words, I spoke with two men who wrote speeches and presentations for the former Chrysler head: Mike Morrison and Alex Tsigdinos. Morrison, Chrysler's vice president of corporate communications from 1984 to 1999, wrote more than 600 of Iacocca's speeches. Tsigdinos, who worked for Morrison, was part of Iacocca's and Chrysler's small speech-writing team during his last few years at the company.

My goal was to discover what lessons could be learned to help today's executives use speeches to help grow their companies in today's still uncertain economy.

Morrison stressed that Iacocca's speaking style and his belief in the value of speeches came from his background in sales. "In the auto industry, sales means talking to dealers," Morrison said. "At that time, dealers were all independent business people, protected by state franchise laws. You couldn't force them to do anything. You had to sell to salesmen, sometimes getting them to do things they didn't want to do."

Iacocca himself put it this way: "In every speech I give the object is to motivate. You can deliver information in a letter or tack it on a bulletin board."

Unfortunately, far too many of today's executives forget the motivational aspect. Most, in fact, prefer to treat a speech as a spoken white paper or a status report to stockholders rather than as an opportunity to rally the troops. The result is a lot of very boring CEO speeches.

Iacocca, on the other hand, planned out each speech very concisely and with great focus, Tsigdinos said, to be sure he would move his audiences to action. "He wanted to know what we wanted to accomplish with each particular audience: the point he wanted to make, the behavior he wanted to influence, the actions he wanted them to take," Tsigdinos explained.

Tsigdinos noted that because Iacocca understood how overwhelmingly important it was to persuade, he put a huge amount of effort into each speech. "He always spoke from a script, never spoke off the cuff," said Morrison. In fact, Iacocca was always very nervous before a speech. However, because he put in the hours to rehearse and revise each speech, his delivery was so smooth, natural, and relaxed, it could sound adlibbed.

"I think some executives think all they need to do is review a draft just before they give it, and they can waltz in there and win an audience over," said Tsigdinos. "Iacocca knew it wasn't that easy."

Check out YouTube for proof that too many executives don't put in the time. You'll find lots of examples of CEOs who read their speeches instead of delivering them.

As for the substance of the speeches, Morrison summed it up simply: "A good speech is a story." In fact, he said, Iacocca knew that everything having to do with communication was a story. "Iacocca was a great at telling stories with a beginning, a strong middle, and an end."

For too many of today's CEOs, a speech is what Morrison called "just a matter of reciting data, of listing serial events." That's a bad mistake that first bores, then ultimately loses an audience.

Iacocca was so devoted to making each speech a story that he didn't want Morrison to add in applause lines. "He didn't want anything to break up the flow of a story," Morrison said, "No cute phrases, not a lot of short anecdotes. He would set up the story, tell it, draw his conclusion, and leave."

And he stayed far away from corporatespeak. Said Tsigdinos, "Simple but effective. That's what we strove for. No convoluted language. He was great at making direct statements that people could remember."

He was also great at taking the initiative and getting out front on issues. In 1987, it was discovered that Chrysler had tested a small number of new cars with the odometers disconnected before they were sold. The story rocketed around the country, and there were reports district attorneys were considering legal action. When Iacocca learned what had happened, he had Morrison draft a speech saying very frankly that Chrysler had made a mistake and would make it right.

When Morrison sent the draft to Chrysler lawyers for clearance, they were furious—fearing the speech could be an admission of guilt and lead to lawsuits. Iacocca was just as furious that the lawyers had tried to stop him.

So when he went before the cameras, he said that Chrysler had done two things that made customers question their faith in the company. In Iacocca's soon-to-be-famous words: "The first was dumb....The second reached beyond dumb and went all the way to stupid."

"He was on every one of the nightly news shows," Morrison remembered. "They lionized him, and he turned the whole thing into a huge PR victory."

There's an obvious contrast to the recent behavior of some CEOs facing crises, most notably BP's. "The BP guys should have understood they had a disaster on their hands. They should have worked with their communication experts, not their lawyers," Morrison said.

As today's CEOs work to keep their companies growing out of the economic doldrums, they would be wise to learn from Lee:

- Use your speeches to motivate, not just deliver information.
- Put in whatever time it takes to master your speech and make it sound natural.
- Get out front, be frank, admit your mistakes.
- And above all—Tell a story!

How Warren Buffett Captures Your Attention

The first thing CEOs must do if they want to inspire confidence through speeches and presentations is make sure their listeners remember their words. Unfortunately, far too many deliver a fog of standard MBA-style buzzwords, which are instantly forgotten.

And then there's Warren Buffett.

Buffett is arguably the most successful and famous investor in the world, so his words would capture attention, no matter what he said or how he said it. However, Australian blogger Ian Whitworth, a creative director and fierce foe of jargon, points out that Buffett rises high above the ordinary. How? The unbelievably successful uber-CEO "knows how to paint a picture with his words. Admittedly, some of those pictures are a little hallucinogenic, but you won't forget them in a hurry."[15]

(15). *"Warren Buffett buzzes nudist camps." Can You Hear Me Up the Back?Tips on creating presentations with personality, http://www.scenechange.com.au/blog/?p=399*

To prove it, Whitworth wrote about several fairly commonplace business situations. He then showed how a regular CEO would describe them, and finally listed the actual Buffett quotes from the Berkshire Hathaway annual message to shareholders.

SITUATION 1: Insurance is one of the few industries with sales growth potential.

Regular CEO:

"We see solid potential upside for insurance product units going forward."

Buffett:

"We're like two hungry mosquitoes in a nudist camp."

SITUATION 2: Unknown exposure to toxic debt means banks don't trust each other at the moment.

Regular CEO:

"Cross-bank debt exchange structures currently exhibit heightened risk variables."

Buffett:

"Participants seeking to dodge troubles face the same problem as someone seeking to avoid venereal disease: It's not just whom you sleep with, but also whom they are sleeping with."

(Note to readers: while you should learn from Buffett, I strongly recommend that you rarely if ever give a speech with the words "nudist" or "venereal" in it.)

What Steve Jobs Knew— About Great Presentations[16]

The outpouring of news stories, and personal reflections after the sad news of Steve Jobs' death focused on the tremendous impact he had, not only on the hi-tech business, but on everyday lives.

However, we shouldn't forget that Jobs may have been the best CEO communicator of our time. (Lee Iacocca is the only one who could give him a run for his money.) Luckily for current CEOs, many of Jobs' best presentations live on, on YouTube and elsewhere on the Web.

The best way for an executive to learn from Jobs is to watch those videos. But here are some lessons to be learned.

Stories. Jobs embodied one of the key pieces of advice I give to clients: Use stories, not statistics. Carmine Gallo, (carminegallo.com), an executive presentation coach who has written a couple books about Jobs, once noted: "Steve Jobs is the world's greatest corporate storyteller. Instead of simply delivering a presentation like most people do, he informed, he educated, he inspired and he entertained, all in one presentation." And he knew that the best stories had tension and even conflict.

Passion. Jobs knew that the way to move an audience (and sell products) was to be passionate. He never just listed the features of the new iPhone or iPad. Instead he spoke excitedly about how they could change people's lives. I'm convinced every CEO should "be like Steve" and look for places where he or she can inject some emotion.

Know your audience. Jobs knew very well what he had to do to hold on to his audience. Some of his presentations were pretty darn long. But he always made sure to break them up with videos, graphics, etc. He also often yielded the stage to other folks from Apple, knowing that an audience will tune out even the best speaker if he or she goes on too long.

Vision. Jobs used the passion in his speeches to connect audiences to a vision. "When he showcased a product, he never confined himself to talking about its cool features," says Khris Baxter, who helps local executives give better presentations. "He always linked the device to a vision of a better life, a connection to the future, or a richer experience." He even used vision to recruit employees, most famously when he asked then-Pepsi President John Sculley, "Do you want to spend your life selling sugar water or do you want to change the world?"

Practice. Practice. Practice. Both Jobs and Iacocca seemed to give their speeches off the cuff, because they seemed so conversational and immediate. In fact, both men were fanatical about rehearsing their presentations—hour after hour—until they had them down cold.

To be honest, I still can't quite believe Steve Jobs is gone. Thanks for wonderful technology, and terrific presentations.

CONCLUSION

Conclusion

The title of the first chapter of this book, "Why Bad Speeches Happen to Good CEOs," is also the title of a workshop I give regularly to executives in the corporate and nonprofit worlds. Those workshops have reinforced a lesson I've learned from my clients: every one can improve the way they use the spoken word. No one comes out of the womb with the ability to give a great speech, but everyone has the ability to learn techniques and approaches that will take their speeches, talks, and presentations to the next level.

I hope this book will be the first step that takes you up to that higher level, and takes your organization to new levels of success.

About Jeff Porro

Jeff Porro is a Washington, D.C. -based speechwriter for Fortune 250 CEOs, diplomats, and other government leaders, as well as executives of some of the nation's leading trade and professional associations. He is also an award winning screenwriter and a PhD with 20 years of experience in research, public policy, and business. He has been profiled in the *Washington Post*, *National Journal*, *Washington Business Journal*, and other publications.

You can reach him at jeff@porrollc.com

And A Special Offer

If you have a speech or talk that you're worried about or that fell short of your goals, send it to me at jeff@porrollc.com.

I'll do a free audit, providing useful suggestions on how to do better.

Made in the USA
Lexington, KY
09 May 2013